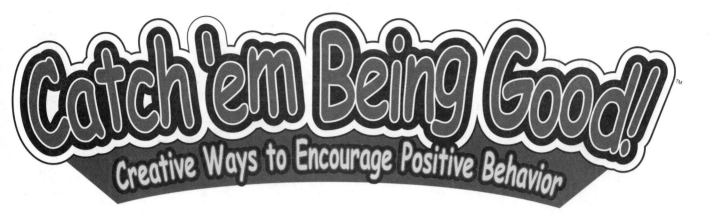

Catch 'em Being Good!
Creative Ways to Encourage Positive Behavior

Editor: Carla Hamaguchi
Illustrator: Darcy Tom
Cover Illustrator: Kimberly Schamber
Designer: Terri Lamadrid
Cover Designer: Barbara Peterson
Art Director: Tom Cochrane
Project Director: Carolea Williams

Table of Contents

Introduction

Promote positive student behavior by catching students being good! Focus on the good things that students do and reinforce those actions with a variety of rewards. *Catch 'em Being Good!* features rewards you can use to acknowledge the achievements of individuals, small groups, and the whole class. Both the small-group and whole-class achievement rewards promote positive peer pressure and camaraderie. You will find ways to maintain a positive learning environment that complements a diverse range of classroom management styles.

Rewarding students doesn't have to be expensive. You'll find several suggestions for no-cost rewards (see page 9) and a whole section of reproducible rewards. Simply copy the reproducibles on colored paper and you'll have a variety of rewards to pass out to students.

If you are looking for more creative reward ideas, turn to pages 45–48. There you'll find several ideas for making your own rewards using everyday teacher supplies such as borders and stickers.

Other fun resources you'll find in this book include
• ideas for bulletin board displays
• reproducible certificates
• individual incentive charts
• reproducible raffle tickets
• reproducible coupons
• ways to reinforce classroom rules

This all-inclusive resource guide makes it easy to implement incentive programs and reward students for their efforts. With all this information at hand, you are ready to Catch 'em Being Good!

Establishing Classroom Rules

Make your classroom rules meaningful and memorable to your class by involving students in the process of generating the rules. During the first days of the school year, brainstorm with students their classroom rights and responsibilities. Based on these rights and responsibilities, discuss acceptable and unacceptable classroom behavior. Then, generate together a set of class rules, keeping the following in mind:

• Keep rules brief.
• Generate broad rules.
• Keep rules few in number.
• Use a positive tone (i.e., tell what to do, rather than what not to do).

Test the usefulness of the rules and establish clear definitions of them by suggesting hypothetical situations in which students demonstrate acceptable and unacceptable behavior. Discuss as a class the rule that applies to each situation. Reword the rules as necessary to make sure all situations are addressed. Finally, number the rules, and post them within all students' view. When students are in violation of a rule, simply hold up the number of fingers that corresponds to the rule to avoid interrupting your lesson or train of thought. Because students were active in creating the rules, they will be much more likely to abide by them. The following is an example of an effective set of rules:

1. Be responsible.

2. Be respectful.

3. Be resourceful.

4. Be a risk-taker.

Class Rule Display Ideas

Create a fun display to show off your class rules. Here are just a few creative ideas.

Keys to Success

Make several copies of the Key reproducible (page 7) on tagboard, and cut them out. Cover the keys with aluminum foil, punch holes in the tops, and string them onto a thick piece of yarn. Use a permanent marker to write a rule on each key. Staple the keys and yarn to a bulletin board titled *Keys to Success!*

Good Bee-havior

Use stickers from Creative Teaching Press's Spring Stickety-Splits (CTP 0647) to create this rebus rules chart.

Catch 'em Being Good

Make enlarged copies of the Fish reproducible (page 8). Write a rule on each fish, and display the fish on a bulletin board as shown. Use construction paper or butcher paper to make a "fishing pole," and attach the pole to the bulletin board. Attach a piece of string to one end of the pole. Explain to the class that you will be looking to "catch" students who are following the rules. Make several copies of the Fish reproducible on colored paper, and cut out the fish. Or, use

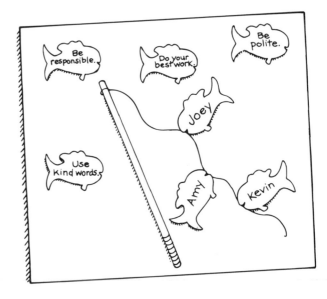

Creative Teaching Press's Fish Calendar Cut-Outs (CTP 4940) or Fish Super Cut-Outs (CTP 4874). Give students a fish when you see them demonstrate good behavior. Have students write their name on their fish, and invite them to place their fish on the string.

Class Constitution

Use a large piece of butcher paper to create a paper scroll. Write the class rules on the scroll, and label the rules *Class Constitution*. Use Creative Teaching Press's Stars Stickety-Splits (CTP 0648) to decorate the scroll. Display the scroll so it is visible to all students.

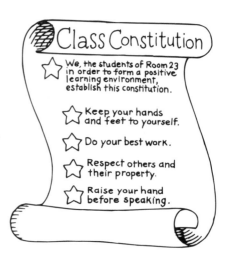

Key

Fish

Establishing Classroom Rules

Reward Ideas

Create a prize box quickly and inexpensively by covering a shoe box with gift wrap, or use Creative Teaching Press's Treasure Chest (CTP 5999). Fill the box with small inexpensive rewards (e.g., stickers, pencils, erasers, bookmarks). Purchase small items, or ask parents to donate items to be used as rewards. Look for items in the birthday party section of discount stores. There are also several no-cost rewards. Copy rewards from the Reproducible Rewards section of this book (see pages 31–44) to create "free time" or "no homework" coupons or passes. Do not forget the free stickers you get in junk mail or from book clubs, and look for coupons from fast food chains.

Rewards
Stickers
Pencils
Erasers
Plastic toys
Plastic jewelry
Certificates
Tickets
Candy
Raisins
Paper
Passes
Parties
Special assemblies, movies, or trips
A picnic

No-Cost Rewards
Be the first in line
Lunch with the teacher
Help make a bulletin board
Free time
No Homework Pass
Be a classroom helper
Draw on the chalkboard
Fast food coupons

Individual Incentive Programs

Use the following ways to recognize individual students who exhibit exemplary behavior:

Cool Coupons

Brainstorm with students privileges or small prizes they would like to earn. Make several copies of the Cool Coupons (page 14). Write some of the students' favorite privileges or prizes on the blank Cool Coupons, and copy the coupons on colored card stock. Cut apart the coupons, and display them in a clear container. Keep a large supply of coupons available to reward students who are staying on task, helping a classmate, or demonstrating appropriate behavior.

Super Behavior Store

Gather pennies, nickels, dimes, and quarters, or make several copies of the Coins and Bills reproducibles (pages 15 and 16). Have students make banks, wallets, or other containers to store the money. Tape an index card to the corner of each student's desk. Whenever you see a student setting a good example, add a tally mark to his or her "point card." Have students meet with you to trade in their points for money. Have students count their points and tell you what coins or dollars they expect to get. For example, a student has 15 points and tells you that he or she should get a dime and a nickel. Then, trade the points for money. Have students collect money for two weeks. Place price tags on small items (e.g., pencils, toys), display the items on a table, and then open the "store." Invite students to make their purchases. Teach proper manners, patience while waiting in line, and the fact that we cannot always afford what we want. Explain how to save for larger purchases. After a few store openings, invite student volunteers to be the cashiers. Give them change and waist aprons or a cash drawer. Invite volunteers to practice making change and selling items.

Raffle Tickets

Make several copies of the Raffle Tickets (page 17) on colored construction paper, and cut them apart. When you want to reward students for accomplishments such as bringing back permission slips or homework on time, helping a classmate, or being a good listener, give them a ticket. Have students write their name on the ticket and place it in a jar. Each week, draw a few winning tickets. Have the winners choose a prize from the prize box (see page 9). Empty the jar each week, or have students accumulate tickets all year.

Reward Chart

Make several copies of the Caught Being Good Tickets (page 18) on card stock. Cut apart the tickets, and store them in an envelope or a plastic bag. Create a list of privileges or prizes with students, and record the number of tickets which must be redeemed to win them on a reward chart. Hand out a ticket when you catch a student exhibiting a behavior that you would like to reinforce. Have students write their name on their tickets and keep them in a safe place. Give rewards on a variable schedule so students never know when they will be rewarded. At the end of the week, give students the opportunity to redeem their tickets for a prize. If students do not have enough tickets to redeem for a prize, they can hold on to them until the following week.

Reward Chart	
Privileges	Tickets Needed
Be first in line	5
No homework	10
Free time	10
Picnic in the park	15

Gold Coin Rewards

Spray wooden nickels or plastic chips with gold paint. Give each student a juice can, and invite him or her to cover this "gold coin container" with colored contact paper. Supervise students as they use a permanent marker to write their name on the can. Invite students to decorate their can with stickers and keep it at their desk or table or in their cubby. Then, as a class, list classroom privileges that can be earned with gold coins (e.g., line up first, choose a book for the teacher to read, eat lunch in the classroom). Look for students who follow classroom rules, use their time wisely, and/or show respect for others, and reward them with a gold coin. At the end of the week, give students the opportunity to redeem their coins for a reward.

Individual Incentive Charts

Give each student a copy of an individual incentive chart (see pages 19–20). Invite students to color their chart and tape it on the corner of their desk or table. Reward students with a small sticker or stamp when they are following directions and are on task. Have students place each sticker in a separate box on their chart. Invite children to choose a reward from the prize box (see page 9) when their grid is completely filled.

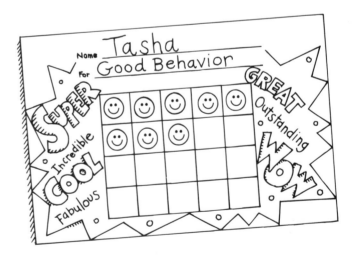

Incentive Cards

Make several copies of the Incentive Cards (page 21) on colored card stock. Cut apart the cards, and give one card to each student. Ask students to write their name on their card and keep it in their desk. When students are caught being good or have completed a homework assignment, hole-punch their card or stamp it with a small rubber stamp. Invite students to choose a prize from the prize box (see page 9) when all the circles on their card have been punched or stamped.

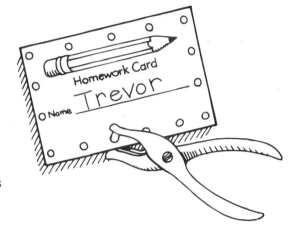

Build a Rainbow

For each student, make an arc of the rainbow in red, orange, yellow, green, blue, and purple construction paper. Make the red arc biggest and the purple arc smallest so that each color is $1/2$" (13 mm) smaller than the previous color. Laminate the arcs if possible. Type each student's name on white paper, cut it out, and tape it on the inside of the plastic of a pocket chart. Place all of the rainbow pieces in a bucket or rainbow bag. When a student sets a good example (e.g., does an act of kindness, takes a learning risk), tell him or her to *Build a rainbow*. Have the student go to the bucket or bag, take out the next color, and place it in front of the previous color to add to his or her rainbow. (You may want to have a completed rainbow on display for students to use as a guide when adding the next appropriate color.) If a student breaks a class rule, have him or her take a color arc away. When students complete their rainbow, reward them with a prize.

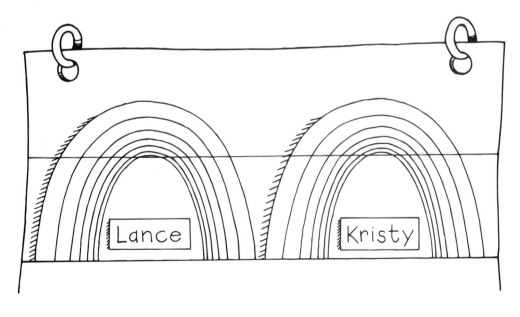

Cool Coupons

First
in Line

Teacher's
Helper

Individual Incentive Programs

Catch 'em Being Good!™ © 2003 Creative Teaching Press

Coins

Bills

Individual Incentive Programs

Raffle Tickets

Ticket	Ticket	Ticket
Ticket	Ticket	Ticket
Ticket	Ticket	Ticket
Ticket	Ticket	Ticket
Ticket	Ticket	Ticket
Ticket	Ticket	Ticket
Ticket	Ticket	Ticket
Ticket	Ticket	Ticket
Ticket	Ticket	Ticket

Caught Being Good Tickets

Caught Being Good	Caught Being Good	Caught Being Good
Caught Being Good	Caught Being Good	Caught Being Good
Caught Being Good	Caught Being Good	Caught Being Good
Caught Being Good	Caught Being Good	Caught Being Good
Caught Being Good	Caught Being Good	Caught Being Good
Caught Being Good	Caught Being Good	Caught Being Good
Caught Being Good	Caught Being Good	Caught Being Good
Caught Being Good	Caught Being Good	Caught Being Good
Caught Being Good	Caught Being Good	Caught Being Good

Individual Incentive Programs

Homework Incentive Chart

Name _____

For _____

Name _____

For _____

Good Job Incentive Chart

Name _____

For _____

SUPER
Incredible
COOL
Fabulous

GREAT
Outstanding
WOW

Name _____

For _____

SUPER
Incredible
COOL
Fabulous

GREAT
Outstanding
WOW

Individual Incentive Programs

Incentive Cards

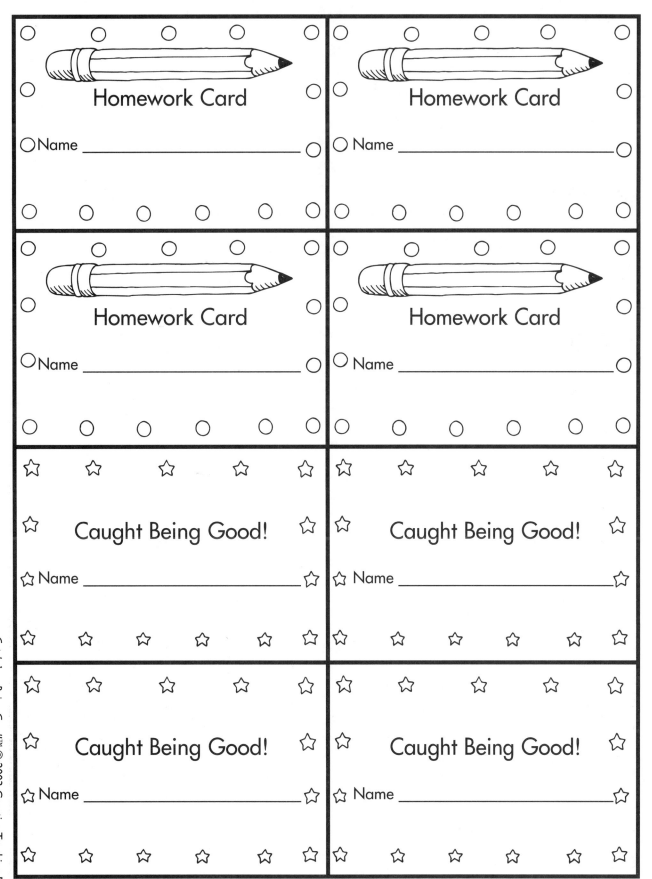

Homework Card

Name _____

Homework Card

Name _____

Homework Card

Name _____

Homework Card

Name _____

Caught Being Good!

Name _____

Caught Being Good!

Name _____

Caught Being Good!

Name _____

Caught Being Good!

Name _____

Small-Group Incentive Programs

Using small groups to encourage on-target student behavior is smart teaching. Peers encourage each other to meet and exceed your expectations and working together towards points or other rewards can bring a group together. Here are a few ways to reward groups who are working well together:

Group Rewards

Draw a large box in the corner of your board, and divide the box so that there is one section for each group in your class. Award points to the first few groups seated, attentive, and prepared for the next lesson following a transition. At the end of each week, give a reward to the three groups with the most points. For example, if you use raffle tickets, give each student in the group with the most points three tickets, each student in the group with the second-most points two tickets, and so on. If you award privileges, consider having lunch with the groups and bringing a dessert treat for each student.

It Takes Teamwork

Have each group generate a name (suggest themes at the start of each new grading period or unit), and write it on a large piece of construction or butcher paper. Invite the groups to decorate their banner, and then display the banners above the groups or on the walls. As students work together, award stickers or stamps to deserving groups on their banner. Count the stickers or stamps at the end of each week, and invite the group that earned the most stickers or stamps (for that week) to take a trip to the prize box (see page 9), or offer some other suitable reward (e.g., no homework coupons, free time).

Stick to It

Photograph each group, and display the pictures on a bulletin board, each with a different color of 9" x 12" (23 cm x 30.5 cm) construction paper stapled beneath it. Add stickers or stamps to the corresponding paper as each group earns recognition. At the end of the week, award a small prize to the three groups with the most stamps or stickers. Change the paper at the end of each week.

Tracking System

Make several copies of the Road, Cars, and Signs reproducibles (pages 24–26). Color and cut apart each road, car, and sign. Display the road, and use the colored cars to track the progress of small groups. Assign a colored car to each group, and write the group names on the cars. Display the cars at the start of the track, and place the road signs along the length of the track. Move the cars along the "road" to each sign to show the groups' progress. For example, if you track group behavior, each time groups behave properly, move their car to the next sign on the road. Reward groups when they reach the end of the road.

Road

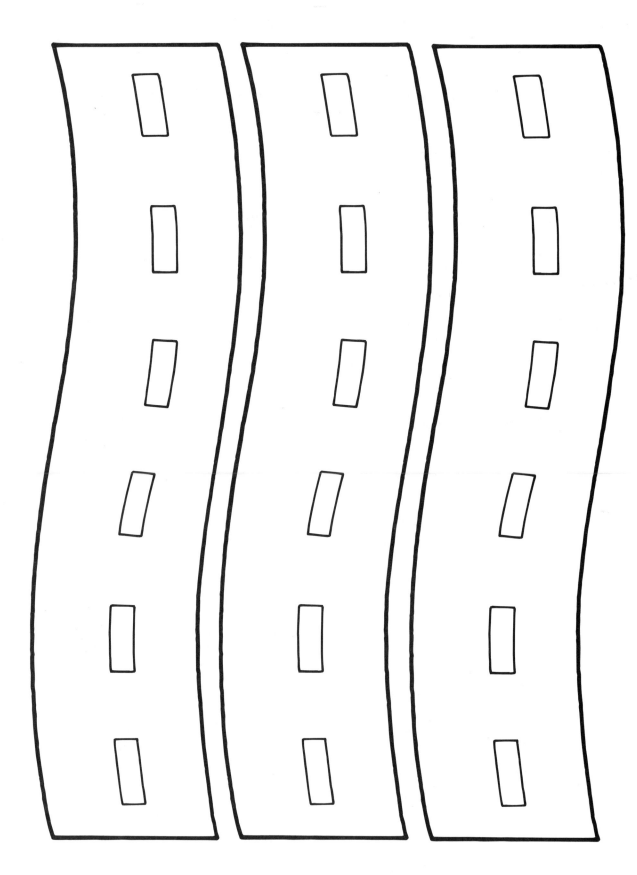

Small-Group Incentive Programs

Cars

Signs

Small-Group Incentive Programs

Whole-Class Incentive Programs

Rewarding a class for a job well done can help encourage individual students to do their best for the benefit of the class and brings the group together to work towards a common goal. Listed below are a few easy-to-implement systems for rewarding a class that is functioning well as a group. For each system, have the class agree in advance on the reward they are working towards (e.g., a pizza party, a movie in class).

First One to the Top

Draw a ladder on a piece of butcher paper. Hang the "ladder" where it is visible to all students. Make a copy of the Footprint reproducible (page 29) on colored construction paper, and cut it out, or use Creative Teaching Press's Footprint Super Cut-Out (CTP 4865). Each time the class exceeds expectations, move the footprint cutout one rung up the ladder. Award a prize when you place the footprint on the top rung. Alternatively, use a real ladder (which has fewer steps), and have the class earn five tally marks before you move the footprint each step.

Paper Chain

Make a paper chain with a link for each point students must earn towards their prize. Hang the chain high enough to keep it safe, but low enough that students can reach it with your help. Every time the class deserves recognition for their behavior, have a student break the next link in the chain. When the last link is broken, give students their reward.

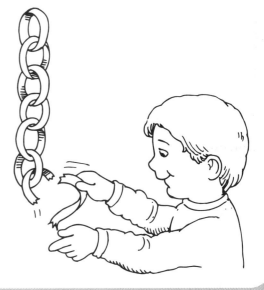

Super Scene

Create a scene representing the reward (e.g., a class picnic) on a bulletin board. At the bottom of the scene, add enough elements (e.g., a picnic basket, a sandwich) for each point the class must earn for the prize. Each time the class deserves recognition for their behavior, have a student move an element into the scene, until all the elements have been moved into the scene and the class earns the reward.

Guess the Phrase

Write on the board a blank line for each letter in the word for the reward (e.g., 10 blank lines for a pizza party). Each time the class is on task, fill in one of the blank lines. When the class completes the phrase, they win the prize.

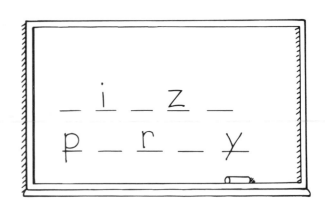

Create a Quilt

Copy the Quilt Square reproducible (page 30) on several pieces of different colored construction paper. Frame a bulletin board with borders. Each time you catch the class being good, write the task (e.g., in line, on task) on a square. Attach the square to the bulletin board display. Continue adding squares to the display until a "quilt" is complete. Reward the class when the quilt is complete.

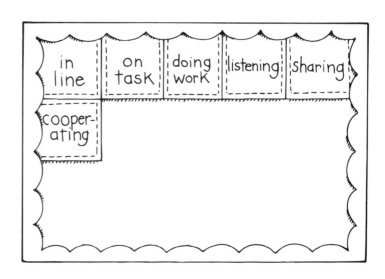

Footprint

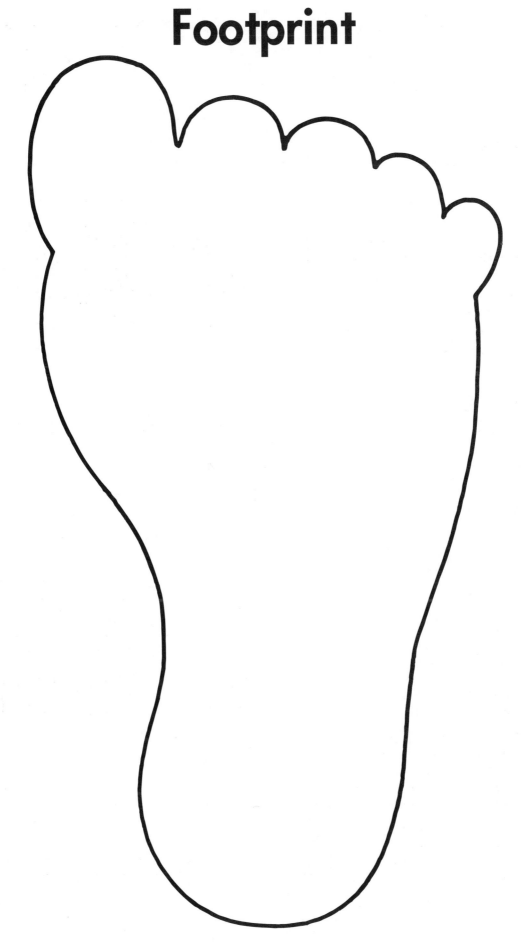

Quilt Square

Whole-Class Incentive Programs

Reproducible Rewards

Making your own rewards can be as simple as copying reproducibles! Copy the reproducibles in this section of the book on colored paper, card stock, or construction paper to make handy rewards!

Pencil Rewards

Copy the Pencil Rewards (page 33) on colored construction paper or colored card stock. Cut out each reward. Use an X-ACTO® knife to cut slits on the X's. Have students slide a pencil though both X's.

Caught Being Good Glasses

Copy the Caught Being Good Glasses reproducible (page 34) on card stock. Invite students to use crayons or markers to color the glasses. Have them cut out the frame and two arms of the glasses. Ask them to carefully cut a slit at "A" and "B" of the frame and arms. Have students attach the arms to the frame by fitting them into the designated slits.

Redeemable Coupons

Copy the reproducible coupons (pages 35–37) on colored construction paper, and cut them apart. Store the coupons in a plastic bag, and have them handy to pass out to students who are caught being good. Personalize the blank coupons (see page 37) by writing the student's name and the reward.

This coupon entitles

Melissa

to

read with a friend

Notes

Copy the Teacher Note and Great Day! Note reproducibles (pages 38–39) on colored paper, and cut the pages in half. Write notes home to parents on the notepaper, and send the notes home with students to inform parents of their children's behavior.

Certificates

Copy the reproducible certificates (pages 40–43) on colored paper or construction paper. Fill in the blanks on the certificates to personalize them for each student. See page 46 for a fun way to present certificates.

Watches

Copy the Watches reproducible (page 44) on card stock, and cut apart the watches. Use an X-ACTO knife to cut slits on the four lines on each watch. When you reward a student with a watch, invite him or her to use crayons or markers to color the watch. Have students place the tab into the appropriate slit to fit the watch onto their wrist.

Pencil Rewards

Caught Being Good Glasses

Reproducible Rewards

No Homework Coupons

No
homework
for

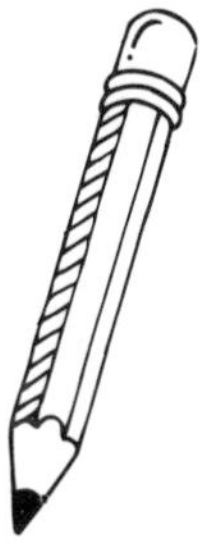

_____

No
homework
for

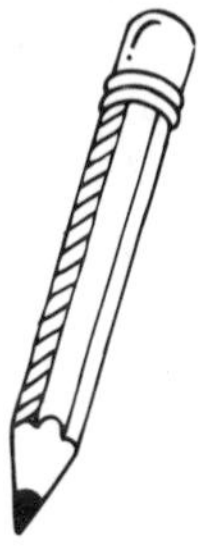

_____

No
homework
for

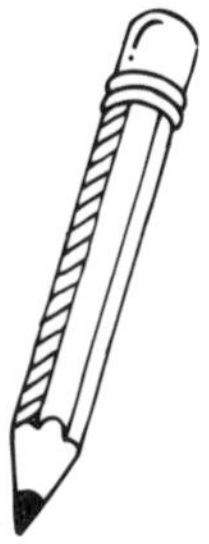

_____

No
homework
for

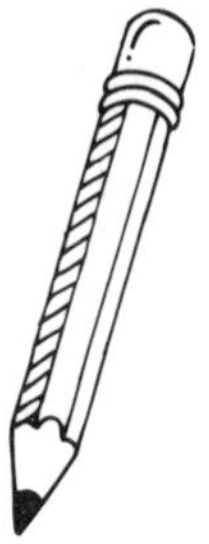

_____

No
homework
for

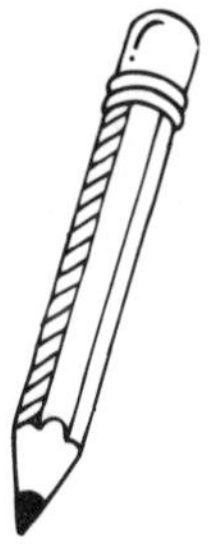

_____

No
homework
for

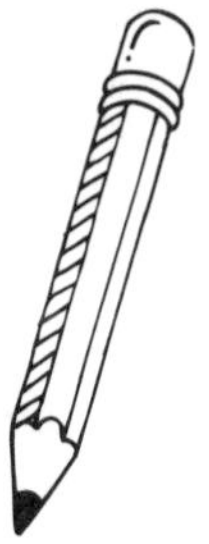

_____

No
homework
for

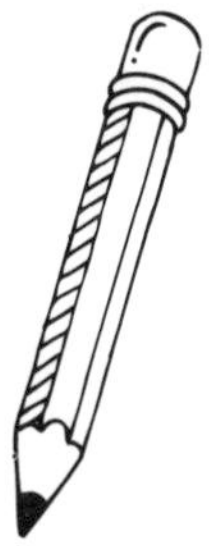

_____

No
homework
for

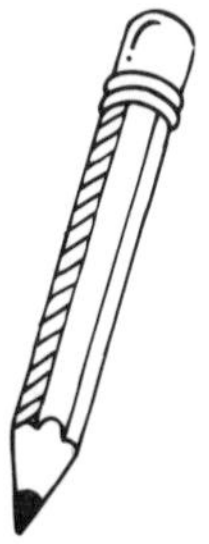

_____

Free Time Coupons

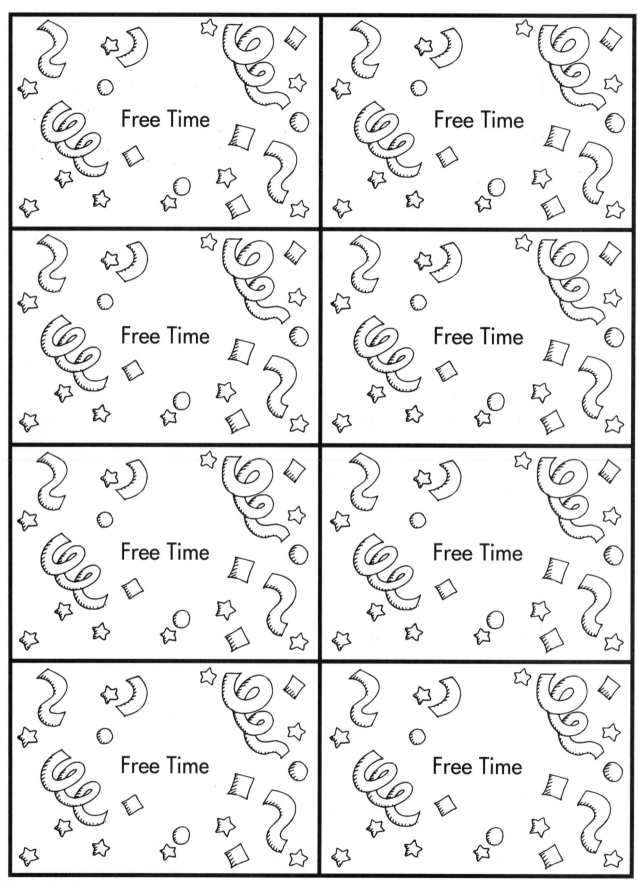

Free Time

Free Time

Free Time

Free Time

Free Time

Free Time

Free Time

Free Time

Reproducible Rewards

Coupons

This coupon entitles

to

This coupon entitles

to

This coupon entitles

to

This coupon entitles

to

Reproducible Rewards

Teacher Note

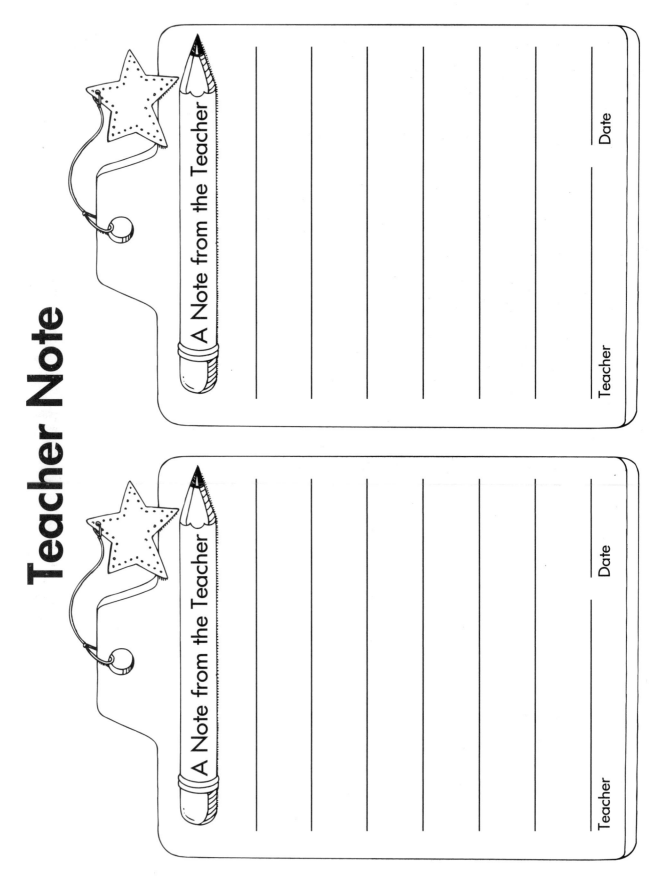

A Note from the Teacher

Teacher _____ Date _____

A Note from the Teacher

Teacher _____ Date _____

Catch 'em Being Good!™ © 2003 Creative Teaching Press

Great Day! Note

_____ had a great day!

_____

_____

_____

_____

Teacher _____

Date _____

_____ had a great day!

_____

_____

_____

_____

Teacher _____

Date _____

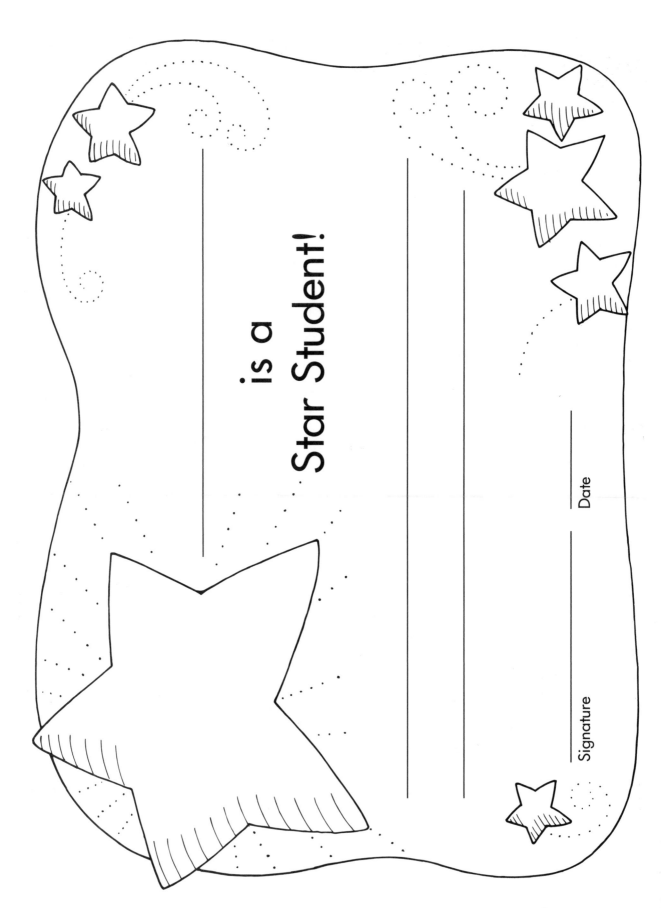

is a
Star Student!

Signature

Date

40

Reproducible Rewards

Remarkable Reader

Congratulations

for

Signature

Date

Certificate of Excellence

Awarded to

_____

for _____

_____

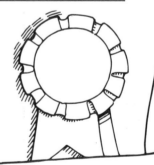

_____ _____
Signature   Date

Brilliant Behavior

for

Signature

Date

Watches

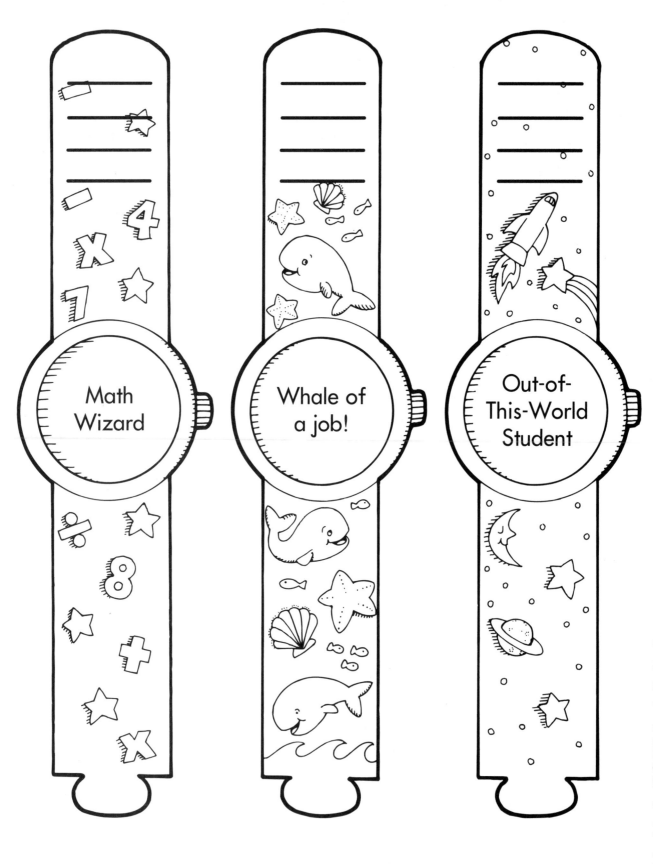

Math
Wizard

Whale of
a job!

Out-of-
This-World
Student

Reproducible Rewards

Make Your Own Creative Rewards

It's fun to use existing decorative products to make appealing three-dimensional rewards for your students. All you need is some of Creative Teaching Press's decorative items and your imagination. Here are just a few easy-to-do ideas to get you started:

Reward Ribbons

Use ribbon and a star sticker from the Stars Stickety-Splits (CTP 0648) or a Perfect Star Calendar Cut-Out (CTP 4815) to create a fun reward.

Decorative Pencil

Wrap a piece of pipe cleaner around one end of a pencil. Attach a star sticker from the Stars Stickety-Splits (CTP 0648) to each end of the pipe cleaner to create this fun pencil topper. Wrap stickers around the pencil to add more decorations.

Pencil Stand

Cut a border into 6" (15 cm) pieces. Fold one piece into fourths. Open the border piece so it is folded in half. Cut a small triangle in the center top of the fold. Glue the two end panels of the border together to create a stand. Decorate the stand with Good Work Stickers (CTP 1809). Invite students to rest their pencil on the stand.

Crowns

Use any of Creative Teaching Press's gingham borders (CTP 0398–0402) or dot borders (CTP 1352–1357) to make "crowns." Fit a border on a student's head. Cut off any excess border, and staple the ends together. Decorate the crowns with Gold Star Stickers (CTP 1804) or Star Calendar Cut-Outs (CTP 4962). Or, use the Gold Stars Border (CTP 0151) to make a star crown.

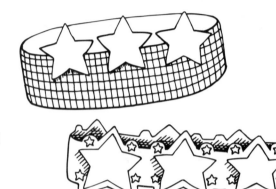

Wrap a Certificate

Cut 1¹/₂" x 6" (3.8 cm x 15 cm) strips of border, and tape the ends together to make small rings. Glue a Star Calendar Cut-Out (CTP 4962) to the ring. Roll up a certificate, and place it in the ring. Make a reading reward by gluing a Book Calendar Cut-Out (CTP 4805) to a ring and placing a copy of the Remarkable Reader Certificate (page 41) in the ring.

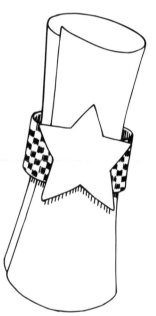

Magnets

Place a piece of magnetic tape to the back of any Calendar Cut-Out or Super Cut-Out to create fun magnet rewards. Write a saying (e.g., Super Work!) on each Cut-Out to personalize the magnets.

Pencil Rewards

Use a hole punch to make two holes in an Apple Super Cut-Out (CTP 4884) as shown. Write on the Cut-Out *A+ Job!* Then, place a pencil in the holes. Use other Super Cut-Outs to create various awards. Here are just a few ideas:

- Write on a Tooth Super Cut-Out (CTP 4871) *I Lost My Tooth* to create a pencil award to give students who lost a tooth.
- Write on a Perfect Star Super Cut-Out (CTP 4832) *Star Student.*
- Write on a Cupcake Super Cut-Out (CTP 4898) *Happy Birthday!*
- Write on a Bear Super Cut-Out (CTP 4899) *Beary Good Behavior.*
- Write on a Whale Super Cut-Out (CTP 4886) *Whale of a Job!*

Organizer Pockets

Give each student a Library Pocket (CTP 1029). Have students write their name on their pocket and use it to store all of their reward tickets and/or coupons.

Bookmarks

Cut any border into 8" (20 cm) sections. Hole-punch each section as shown. Place curling ribbon or yarn through the hole, and tie a knot to attach the ribbon or yarn to the border.

Mini Incentive Charts

Tie a piece of string to each student's desk. Use a clothespin to attach a Super Cut-Out to the string. Reward students with a Hot Spot sticker when you catch them being good. Ask students to place the sticker on their Cut-Out. Invite students to choose a prize from the prize box (see page 9) when they have ten stickers. The following is a list of some of the coordinating Cut-Outs and Hot Spot stickers:

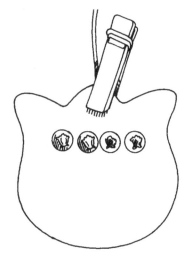

Whale (CTP 4886) or Fish (CTP 4874) Super Cut-Outs and Ocean Hot Spots (CTP 0886)
Apple Super Cut-Outs (CTP 4884) and Apples Hot Spots (CTP 0897)
Star Super Cut-Outs (CTP 4896) and Stars Hot Spots (CTP 0904)
Heart Super Cut-Outs (CTP 4891) and Hearts Hot Spots (CTP 0895)
Tulip Super Cut-Outs (CTP 4857) and Tulips Hot Spots (CTP 0891)
Book Super Cut-Outs (CTP 4822) and Books Hot Spots (CTP 0896)
Smiley Face Super Cut-Outs (CTP 4873) and Smiling Faces Hot Spots (CTP 0918)

Fishing Pole Reward

Attach a piece of string to a pencil. Place a fish sticker from the Ocean Stickety-Splits (CTP 0649) on one end of the string. Attach a paper cutout fish to the other end of the string. Write *Caught Being Good!* on the cutout. Now you have a "fishing pole reward" to hand out to students.

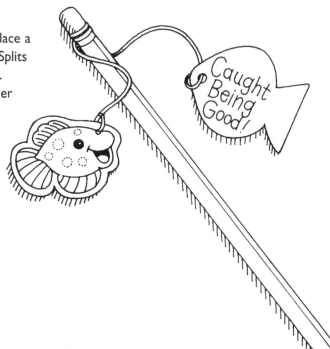

Make Your Own Creative Rewards